I0466633

DEAD
TRUE CRIME

2

GHOUL
OF GRAYS HARBOR

Murder and Mayhem in the Pacific Northwest

C.J. MARCH

SLINGSHOT
BOOKS

San Francisco/Aberdeen, WA, 1900

The British merchant ship drifted slowly toward the rising sun as the crew worked to furl the sails before dropping anchor in San Francisco Bay. The sailors had been at sea for nearly a year, living on salted beef and weevil-infested biscuits. Poorly ventilated, their tiny quarters were fetid, stinking of sweat, tobacco juice, and urine. The floors were wet with spittle. Their clothes were soaked with salt spray and never dried, and scurvy had taken its toll. Bunkmates snapped teeth out of rotted gums and bled from open sores. As the strength of the crew waned, the captain worked them harder.

It was against the law to disobey a ship's officer's orders, and captains could beat or imprison a sailor at their discretion. There was no place to escape to on the open sea. In 1886, the Supreme Court ruled that the Thirteenth Amendment, which abolished slavery and involuntary servitude, did not apply to sailors.

In the past few weeks, it had gotten worse as the captain took to "running out the men"—assigning meaningless and back-breaking work and serving small rations of the most rotted food—in order to make the crew miserable when they reached harbor. If the men deserted the ship, he wouldn't have to pay them their wages. He knew he could count on the "runners" to entice the sailors off his schooner.

The Whitehall boats were already converging on the

vessel, a couple of men in each skiff rowing vigorously. As they closed in, the men hauled out boat hooks and ropes and attached to the schooner, drifting with it into the bay. Climbing up the lines, the runners were ready with bottles of liquor and promises of a warm bed, women, and good food. Many of the sailors took the bottles eagerly, not questioning what they actually contained. Grabbing their duffels, they followed the runners down into the boats. Others weren't convinced and were forced at gunpoint into the Whitehalls.

Before the captain ordered the anchor to drop a mile from shore, the majority of his crew was already headed to the Barbary Coast. Some of the sailors were taken to a saloon where Billy Gohl waited. The building was up on pilings over the harbor. The "crimp" surveyed the sailors, considered the ships in the bay that needed crews, and gave the runners $3/man. The liquor given to the sailors was a mixture of cheap whiskey, brandy, and gin laced with opium. Many of the men were already unsteady on their feet.

Gohl guided one of them to the back of the bar over a hinged flap of wood in the floor. Pressing the release, the man fell through the "dead drop" into a rowboat floating under the saloon. A man in the launch emptied the pockets of the sailor and, with the go-ahead from Gohl, rowed him out to one of the anchored schooners. When the man woke up days later, he would be out at sea. He had been "shanghaied."

The term *shanghai* likely came from the long and dangerous voyage from San Francisco to Shanghai, China. Any sailor unlucky enough to be on the trip was said to have been shanghaied. The meaning of the word evolved to connote kidnapping. Everyone profited from the practice, except the sailor himself.

When a sailor committed to a ship, he received two months' advance salary. Sailors needed to outfit themselves, often at shops that charged inflated prices and provided kickbacks to the captains. He wouldn't get the remainder of his pay until the voyage was complete. If he deserted, he forfeited his entire pay for a trip that lasted anywhere from a couple of months to several years. By "running the men out" or refusing shore leave, captains encouraged desertion to save money on wages.

But then the captain needed a new crew. The runners and crimps were always there with new sailors. Some shipowners, politicians, and police considered it an unsavory but necessary activity. Most treated it as a business—a way to cut costs or make money. The practice flourished well into the twentieth century and was most prevalent in San Francisco, in the neighborhood known as the Barbary Coast, after the pirate-infested waters of North Africa.

In colonial times, sailors were considered first-class citizens, the "first and finest employ," but by the nineteenth century they were "classed with criminals and prostitutes." Politicians and the public had little sympathy for their plight. Because conditions were so awful and wages so meager, it had become impossible to attract native-born Americans. So most were migrants and unable to vote. They were tricked into duty and then beaten, starved, and imprisoned at the discretion of the captain, before returning to port only to be shanghaied onto another voyage.

Shanghaiing was so ubiquitous that the most famous traffickers had names like Shanghai Brown, Shanghai Johnson, and the Shanghai Chicken. The runners would bring the sailors to boarding houses to the crimp who provided the ship with their new crews. Most of the boarding houses were old warehouses built on wooden pilings, with "dead-falls" in the floor through which the sailors were dropped into rowboats. Some crimps made as much as $50,000 a year after paying their runners up to $500 each a week. In today's dollars, that's over $1,000,000. It wasn't until 1906 that shanghaiing became illegal—a result of sailors unionizing. Despite that law, the practice continued.

Billy Gohl got good at shanghaiing.

With wide-set blue eyes and dark hair parted down the middle in bartender fashion, Gohl was striking. In a time when many men had mustaches and beards, he was clean-shaven. Though 6'2" and 200 lb., his barrel chest and thick build made him look shorter. There were rumors about his past, some of which he was more than happy to brag about when he was drinking.

Photograph of Billy Gohl.

Born in Germany on February 6, 1873, he carried around his German accent his entire life. Gohl was suspected of murdering someone in his youth. A fugitive, he fled to Australia. The story of his early life changed depending on who you asked and getting actual details about that first murder was difficult. From Australia, he caught a ride on a ship to Alaska and started a mining venture with a partner. The reward for going into business with Billy Gohl was to become the second man he killed. Depending on the night, Gohl claimed it was an accident or self-defense.

He told more than one person that he ate a man during a cold snap near Whitehorse in the Yukon territory. After his outlaw days in Alaska, he settled down for two years in Montana and married. It's hard to imagine that his bride knew about his man-eating—at least not before the wedding. They had a son together, but one day, Gohl announced he had business in San Francisco and disappeared. She waited two years, but the woman finally had him declared dead, and she remarried. Their son only figured out who his father was long after Billy Gohl was dead.

The San Francisco Gohl found at the turn of the century was exploding. In 1848, before the Gold Rush, the city's population was under a thousand, and fewer than ten ships dropped anchor in the bay that year. Within ten years, though, the population had grown to over fifty thousand. When Gohl arrived forty years later, there were over three hundred thousand people living in San Francisco and over a thousand ships a year made port. The discovery of gold touched off the largest peacetime migration the nation had ever seen.

⊂⊃⊂⊃⊂⊃

The city was a dangerous place, and its most dangerous neighborhood was the Barbary Coast, a nine-block area, much of which is now in modern-day Chinatown. Along with nightsticks and pistols, police carried foot-long knives for chopping off hands in close-quarters fighting. There was at least one account of a man getting decapitated by a police officer.

The policemen worked the streets of Front, Battery, Davis, Drum, and East (now the Embarcadero) in pairs for protection. The crime of the harbor and the saloons and brothels reached the eastern ends of Jackson, Pacific, and Washington streets. There were as many as twenty-three different criminal gangs working the neighborhood at the turn of the century, robbing and raping and kidnapping and killing. Gohl fit in just fine.

In 1885, fifteen years before Gohl arrived, three hundred sailors met on the lumber wharves on Folsom Street. There had been attempts to organize before, but that night 222 of those sailors formed the union that later became the Sailors' Union of the Pacific (SUP). The next year, they staged their first strike. It was a disaster. Shipowners easily crewed their ships with strikebreakers and then blackballed union members. But conditions continued to be abysmal and the trend toward unionization was increasing. The union was able to grow its ranks and expand its tactics.

Gohl joined the SUP in San Francisco and made a name for himself. He heard of a ship in the harbor crewed with nonunion sailors and said he would take care of it. He befriended one of the crewmen and then headed out to the ship. Giving the man's name, Gohl was allowed onboard. Then he took his "friend" hostage and demanded the crew gather on the deck. After disarming the men, he forced them into his launch and took them to the dock in front of the union hall, where they were beaten by union members.

Still, San Francisco was a big and dangerous pond for a little fish like Billy Gohl, tough as he was. There was lots of competition for supremacy in the Barbary Coast underworld. If Billy was going to be the big fish, he'd have to find a smaller pond to work his racket.

The population explosion in San Francisco demanded building materials, and nearly all the schooners loaded with lumber came from a town in Washington. Aberdeen, with a population of ten thousand, was the most productive lumber region in the world at the beginning of the twentieth century. Its founding father, Sam Benn, said that "at the turn of the century, most port towns were wide open, but Aberdeen was 'wider than most.'"

Billy Gohl knew an opportunity when he saw it.

S tepping onto one of the dozen docks in Grays Harbor, Billy Gohl surveyed the port of Aberdeen. The water was bank to bank with three- and four-masted schooners, waiting to be loaded with lumber. Logging camps covered the hillsides of fir, hemlock, cedar, and spruce. The place smelled of cut wood.

Built where the Chehalis and Wishkah Rivers met, Aberdeen kissed the water. Flanked by the cronies he'd convinced to sail with him from San Francisco, Gohl stepped off the dock and into town, seeing opportunity everywhere. Walking along the planks laid over sawdust that formed the town's sidewalks, he took note of the businesses. At a place called the Modern European Lunch Counter, men could buy liquor right from their own boats. The southwest wind pushed the tide; under his feet, the boards closest to the shore rose and settled over the water. The street pulsed beneath him.

Photograph of Aberdeen. Early 1900s.

The buildings sat on pilings. Most were false-front, wood-frame structures and a few, built lower to the ground, had tidewater lapping onto their floors. He counted over twenty-four saloons. He eyed one in particular. Painted red, the Grand Saloon hung over the Wishkah River. A perfect place to install a trapdoor.

Entering one of the dance halls, he found a piano player pounding the keys behind a protective wire screen. A sign stated that "The man that pays the dollar is the one that calls the tune." Gohl watched the lumberjacks in their "tin pants" and wide suspenders throw down whiskey and periodically hurl an empty glass at the pianist.

Nearly two-thirds of Aberdeen were men. Ninety percent were "unmarried drifters" who moved from camp to camp. Gohl learned that they made around twenty cents/hour and worked over thirteen hours a day. Gohl was looking for something with a little more money and a lot less work.

He met Lars Kingstad and opened a cigar store on South

F Street as he settled in and got the lay of the land. Ships in Aberdeen had the same problem as those in San Francisco. They needed crews and this was something Gohl had some experience in.

Commandeering the Grand Saloon down the street from the cigar shop, Gohl had the owner, Ed Dolan, keep a batch of special liquor for men Gohl identified as good candidates for the "misery" ships. Gohl plied the trade he learned in San Francisco, but his ambitions were larger. Aberdeen was going to be his town.

◯━◯━◯

Fire Chief E.L. Koehler was painting the side of his house when he noticed black smoke pouring out of the windows of the Mack Building. Before he had the time to descend the ladder, flames were consuming the structure and had jumped to the L.W. Walker saloon and the Olympus, a "variety house." The flames devoured the buildings, continued down the street and reached the jail and fire hall. Wooden frames and walls collapsed into ash as the Smits Drug Company, the Aberdeen State Bank, and the Central School caught on fire. With their own fire department unable to stop the conflagration, Aberdeen called on the towns of Hoquiam, Montesano, and Cosmopolis for help.

Three men died and 140 buildings burned in the fire of 1903. Daniel Webster worked at the L.W. Walker saloon and jumped from a window. He died two hours later from his injuries in the Aberdeen General Hospital. Samuel Kirkup, a tenant in the Mack Building and a veteran of the Mexican–American War, died in his room. And George Rolf, a man with a peg leg who once ran a cigar stand in competition with Gohl, burned to death in the fire. No one suspected Gohl.

○–○–○

I n 1904, Billy Gohl was elected the Aberdeen agent of the SUP, becoming the union representative for the sailors shipping in and out of Grays Harbor. The port was of such importance to the region and the union so central to commerce that news of his new position was covered in the San Francisco newspapers. He made the new SUP office upstairs at the Grand Saloon. This was one of the first union hiring halls on the Pacific coast.

Not only did he act as the sailor's rep, he was also their banker, often holding onto their money while they were out at sea and paying it out to them like an allowance while they were in port. He knew who had money and who didn't.

The following year, Billy Gohl wandered into a saloon, drunk. He saw a pretty "dance hall girl" and made a pass at her. For his trouble, the woman punched Gohl in the jaw, knocking him down. Then she kicked him in the ribs. If she'd been a man, she probably would have ended up in Grays Harbor. Instead, he married her. Bessie Hager, twenty-seven to Gohl's thirty-two, was the love of Billy's life and his trusted conspirator.

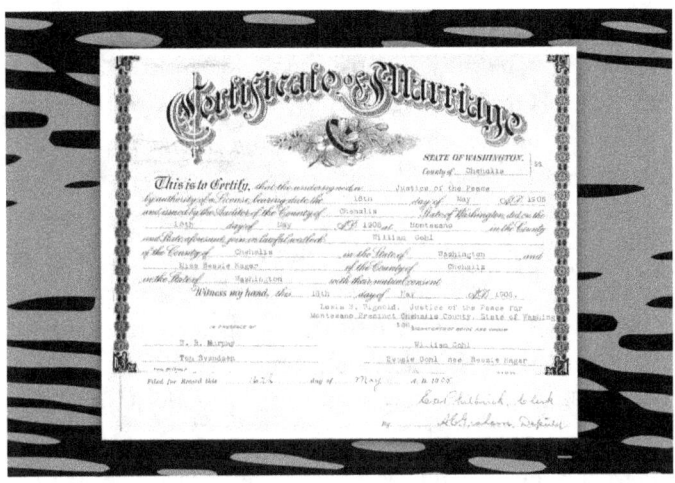

Billy and Bessie's marriage certificate. 1905.

Fittingly, she was a cousin of Frank and Jesse James. Their home was adorned with pictures of the outlaws. When he was drunk, and sometimes when he was sober, he would brag about his relationship to the "James boys of Missouri" and said that he would become just as notorious.

Gohl was assembling his own gang, including men like A.W. Jakobbsen, John Hoffman, John Klingenberg, Charles Hadberg, and Lauritz Jentzen, all of whom would play a role in his undoing. Both Hoffman and Hadberg were German immigrants in their midtwenties. Hadberg was a large man, and the tattoo on his arm of a rose pierced by a dagger with the initials H.H. underneath was familiar to anyone who worked a ship with him. Klingenberg was Danish, though newspapers would call him Norwegian in error, and "slight," 5'4" by some accounts. Hadberg and Klingenberg were sailors, periodically shipping out on the lumber ships. Hoffman was a cigar dealer who worked for Gohl in Aberdeen, and Jakobbsen owned a saloon in town. Lauritz Jentzen, known as "the Weasel," was "in on virtually all of Gohl's escapades."

His "band of thugs" did his bidding, including acting as his alibi when he got in trouble and, in some cases, taking the fall for his crimes. When Gohl was charged with stealing automobile blankets from A.L. Davenport, Hadberg stepped in and told the police that it was him, not Gohl, who had stolen them—despite the fact that the blankets were found in a shack belonging to Gohl. He also used the men when "he desired to accuse an enemy of an offense."

But his crimes only started at stolen goods. He was killing sailors and taking their money, dropping their bodies through the trapdoor in the second floor of the Grand Saloon. While the sailor was putting his money in the open safe, Gohl would knock him unconscious with a "belaying pin" then drag the stunned man to the trapdoor, dropping his body into the boat below. It was quieter than shooting the sailor and saved on bullets.

Some sailors he killed, some he shanghaied. When asked about disappeared men, he said they had shipped out, long gone crewing a lumber schooner. When a dead man washed up, Gohl, as the SUP agent, was usually the one called to identify the body. And the one responsible for forwarding remaining pay to the sailor's family.

He shot one man from the window of the SUP office, bragging "I shot the son-of-a-bitch from my office with my Winchester. I bet that scab won't cross me again." Once, at the end of a pistol, he forced four nonunion sailors out into the bay to a spit called Moon Island that was "bare only at low water" and left them to drown. "I rowed away and I could hear them yelling and splashing about as the water came up over the ground. I had a big laugh, for all of them had told me they couldn't swim." With neither enough evidence nor enough will to tie him to the murders, Billy Gohl's power and brazenness mounted.

Then, down the coast, a natural disaster of epic proportions smote his old stomping ground. It was 1906 and San Francisco shook, then burned.

3

"**S**an Francisco is gone," Jack London wrote of the great San Francisco earthquake and resulting fires. He didn't want to write about the disaster, didn't want to profit from such misery, but the twenty-five cents a word *Collier's* magazine paid him to write the article was the most the great western writer would ever see for his work in his lifetime. In deep debt, London couldn't refuse. But he wasn't the only one grasping at opportunity in the face of disaster.

In the spring of 1906, the earthquake brought to a head the long-simmering tensions between shipowners and sailors. Wages had risen during the disaster for nearly everyone except sailors. The head of the SUP decided to use the crisis to demand a wage increase. The owners refused and sailors walked off, leaving seventy-seven steam schooners empty in San Francisco Bay the first day of the strike. Some owners buckled quickly, giving in to the union demands to crew their ships, but most held out, using nonunion crews. The SUP used strong-arm tactics to press their cause. As a steward of the SUP, Gohl led the efforts in Aberdeen to make sure all ships leaving port were crewed with union sailors. He used the rising hostilities in the wake of the worst disaster in U.S. history at the time to escalate his tactics.

Armed with a pair of revolvers, Gohl took to boarding the streetcars coming from Hoquiam and searching for firearms. The police failed to "check the practice," allowing Gohl to hassle passengers. On the Aberdeen Trades Council, where he represented the sailors' union, he "advocated the burning of the mills of the city, to an extent that made self-respecting, law-abiding members of the council object to sitting with him."

He threatened A. Rupert, manager of West & Slade Grocery Company, and W.B. Mack, manager of the S.E. Slade Lumber Company, and plotted to blow up Mack's house with dynamite because the man refused to meet strikers' demands. It was only the presence of Mack's wife at home that deterred the man Gohl sent. The fate of the failed assassin is unknown, but it's possible the man ended up another of Gohl's victims.

By summer, every paper in Grays Harbor "was filled with his lawless doing." The public was beginning to wonder if the police were afraid of him or if he was being protected by higher-ups. The events of the following year would only increase the speculation. Prominent citizens took to carrying revolvers for protection.

Gohl continued to rob and kill. The schooner *R.C. Slade* was ransacked while docked across the river from Gohl's office. Guns and ammunition were stolen from Frank Becker's sporting goods store. Countless men lost their lives or freedom to the water.

Chehalis River. 1900s.

The sun was setting on the Chehalis and Wishkah Rivers in August 1906. The two-masted schooner, *Fearless*, had sunk anchor in the lower harbor, shortly to cross over and set sail with a load of lumber. Captain C.W. Liljiquist, who lived in Aberdeen, got word that his wife was ill and climbed into a boat to head to shore to check on her. He charged three sailors to watch over the vessel and crew while he was gone. He had reason to worry. There was a nonunion sailor onboard, and Gohl had stormed the ship just a few months earlier in June while the crew was preparing to depart for Mexico. There had been a nonunion sailor onboard then too. The gun battle that ensued caused Liljiquist to be wary of Gohl. The SUP agent had heard that the *Fearless* again had a scab hoisting the mainsail.

No sooner had Liljiquist made shore than Gohl and sixteen of his henchmen loaded into the *Waterboy*, a launch, and rowed out to the *Fearless*. Armed with rifles, they were prepared to remove the nonunion sailor from the ship by any means necessary.

One of the watchmen fled the ship, heading for shore in a small boat. Another schooner in the harbor was moored nearby, its hawser invisible to the sailor in the dark. The cable caught the boat's small mast and overturned the craft, sending the watchman into the water as a man watched from the dock. Vance Baker's drowned body was found in the Chehalis a few days later.

Following gunfire in the harbor, the chief of police was called at 10 p.m. When the chief arrived, Gohl and his men were still onboard, claiming the authority of the SUP. They had searched the schooner and threw all the guns and ammunition they found overboard. The remaining two watchmen were nowhere to be found, rumored to have deliberately left the ship to permit the attackers to board. More than 150 shots were fired.

Only days later, Gohl took eight men armed with rifles and boarded the *Watson A. West*, capturing two nonunion sailors and warning others "they would be severely dealt with." A squad of police waited for them in boats on the lower harbor, but Gohl and his men landed on another shore and stole back to the city by car. Police guarded the raided vessel against another attack.

Longshoremen soon refused to work on any ship against which the SUP had a grievance. Deckhands were quitting, claiming the work too hard. Shipping was "severely handicapped" and labor was in great demand. According to the *San Francisco Call*, "there is not a vessel in port, loading or unloading, but that there is a feeling of stress."

With the police in Aberdeen ineffective against Gohl's crimes, the state took up the case and issued arrest warrants for the attack on the *Fearless*. Ship captains and locals thought that this arrest might spell the end of Gohl's tyranny. But

Gohl was heavily involved in the elections and, through intimidation and bribery, installed many of his cronies into political office.

The preliminary hearing before Justice Fox in the superior court was on August 28, less than a month after the *Fearless* incident and days after Gohl and his men boarded the *Watson A. West*. Charged with "assembling men under arms," Gohl was released on a bond of $500, paid by the SUP. He was the only witness for the defense. Captain Liljiquist and four of his crew took the stand for the prosecution.

A couple of months later, the SUP came to an agreement with the shipowners and the strike ended. The case against Gohl eventually ended in a $1,250 fine that was also paid by the SUP. Gohl resumed his reign over Aberdeen and the shipyards. The next spring, he even ran for fourth vice president of the Washington Federation of Labor.

Gohl had a visible enough standing in the community that his activities were covered in the Tales of the Town Tersely Told section of the *Aberdeen Herald*, from his travels to Tacoma on business to a bout of blood poisoning during the summer of 1907.

With some of his henchman in political office, many of the authorities in his pocket, and the result of his "penitentiary offense" simply a fine paid by the union, Gohl considered himself invincible. The harbor would fill with the dead because of it.

Captain Mersich of the stern-wheeler *Skookum* came across Askel Johnson's body in early February of 1907. Weeks later, John Anderson, a native of Finland, was found dead near Wilson Mill. Then Gus Lindros and Robert Priest and J.B. Meers and Connie Lockett and Gabrielle Austad. Aberdeen earned the nicknames "Hellhole of the Pacific" and "Port of Missing Men."

Over the next eight months, forty-three men were found

floating in Grays Harbor. Some had been shot, others had been poisoned. Most drowned after "falling or being pushed" into the water or being dropped through Gohl's trapdoor. In one month alone, fourteen bodies were pulled out of the harbor. The dead were given the name "floater fleet." During Gohl's time in Aberdeen, this "fleet" numbered 150. Investigators attributed the majority of these deaths to Billy Gohl, making him one of the most prolific murderers in history.

4

Burning down the buildings of his enemies had always worked for Billy Gohl. He'd never been caught so decided to do it again in 1908, to "burn out a saloon man named Lee Williams against whom he had a grudge." He used what newspapers called an "infernal machine," the details of which have been lost to history. Based on Gohl's boast of his dark deed, the contraption, which he called a "patented invention," may have been little more than creative wiring and a long extension cord.

"I used electricity to set it off," he bragged. "I had the damnedest time. I fastened the cord to his light circuit, but the son-of-a-bitch hadn't paid his light bill, and it was turned off. I had to run a wire in from clear across the street to make it go."

His former cigar stand was also in the building and going through bankruptcy. He had reported a stock of cigars to the court that no longer existed, and fire conveniently consumed the empty cigar boxes. His arson killed two birds with one stone.

Gohl brazenly set the fire in broad daylight. Starting it at 2 p.m., he nearly burned down Aberdeen again. The flames in the back of the Alaska saloon on F Street were spotted by Officer Dean who notified the fire department. The fire engine arrived before the water was turned on and the blaze spread into the blacksmith shop next door. The fire quickly moved to the buildings on both sides of the street, destroying the entire block and taking out the Brunswick Hotel. Cinders flew all over East Aberdeen.

The fire engine's stoker refused to maintain a head of steam. Both the Slade and Wilson mills were suddenly in danger. Both mills immediately shut down, sent their combined three hundred workers to fight the fire, and added their "fire apparatus" to the battle. W.B. Mack, manager of the S.E. Slade Lumber Company, turned on the water curtains that were part of the sprinkler system. They barely touched the blaze.

The fire department worked in "a sort of headless, helpless way, apparently not knowing where to contest the flames or what to do." It was only an unusually weak western wind that saved the mills, and the fire burned itself out before reaching them. Four saloons, two blacksmith shops, a small house, a livery barn, and a storage building were completely destroyed. The Alaska saloon and all of its contents were burned to the ground.

Gohl was also rewarded with the incidental death of another enemy. George Griswold, "a well known character in the redlight district," was staying in the Brunswick Hotel and burned to death in his room. Griswold, forty-two years old, as described by the newspaper, "for a number of years has been addicted to the use of morphine, and eked out a precarious existence as porter."

Gohl could consider himself responsible for a new building code. After two massive fires since Gohl had moved to Aberdeen, the city council passed an action to "prohibit the erection of any but first class brick buildings."

Gohl was not arrested for the arson or the death of Griswold, adding to the perception of his invincibility. Now responsible for "fires by the dozens" and nearly burning down

Aberdeen twice, the man remained untouched in his SUP office.

The businessmen of Aberdeen were getting fed up with Gohl and the damage he had done to their businesses and livelihoods, but there appeared little they could do.

○─○─○

While Gohl's reputation with shipowners worsened, many sailors considered him to be a dogged advocate. When a member of the crew of the *Soquel* was assaulted near the American Mill while in harbor, Gohl used it as an excuse to go after the ship's captain, perhaps simply as a show of union strength. He complained to federal authorities that Captain Henningsen wasn't a citizen and therefore couldn't captain an American ship. The charge resulted in an investigation by a United States naturalization examiner.

Considering it "peculiar," Gohl also looked into the wreck of the *Charles E. Falk* against the Copalis Rocks, twelve miles north of Grays Harbor. Contacting the Department of Justice, he requested an investigation, charging its captain and first mate with careless navigation. He criticized Captain Jacobsen and First Mate Holmes for forcing the "tired, wet and hungry sailors" to march two miles to camp in an old barn instead of quartering them at a nearby hotel. Uninsured, the ship was eventually sold at auction.

For these activities, he earned the loyalty of many sailors; sailors who likely had no idea that he would just as soon shanghai or kill them.

Then, in 1909, the Aberdeen Ship Chandlery Company on Wishkah Street made itself a target. According to Gohl, the company was interfering with commissions he had been receiving for supplying ships in Grays Harbor. Gohl decided to burn the place down. He took the entire Zelasko block with it. A logger named Jesse Holcomb perished in the blaze. Another incidental victim. A can with oil-soaked rags was found near the source of the fire, suggesting that Gohl didn't use the "infernal machine" this time. Again, Gohl escaped arrest.

A black man, the owner of a bathhouse destroyed in the fire, was charged instead. Charles Beasley made the mistake of increasing his insurance ten days before, a reasonable action considering the spate of arson in Aberdeen in recent years. Beasley's attorneys were Wilson Buttner and E. E. Boner. Buttner would briefly serve as Gohl's lawyer and Boner would later go on to prosecute Gohl. The two "made a strong effort" and were able to convince the judge that there was insufficient evidence to convict Beasley. Gohl couldn't resist bragging to his cronies about the arson.

Not everyone was intimidated by Gohl. The *Aberdeen Herald* was a frequent critic of corruption and put Gohl in its crosshairs, writing that he was accused of crimes

from petty larceny to piracy to murder to an extent that causes amazement in a civilized community and reflects no credit upon the peace officers of this city and county during that time. Posing as a union labor leader and controller of votes, he apparently found favor in the eyes of crooked politicians and office seekers, too keen for office to be finicky about the means employed to secure it, and through this bunch he acted with apparent immunity from all fear of violated laws.

Gohl didn't like the way that the *Aberdeen Herald* covered him and the SUP, or that police were investigating his operations. He announced that he was moving the headquarters of the SUP from Aberdeen to Hoquiam due to the "antagonistic spirit displayed toward union men in Aberdeen." Hoquiam, a "sister city" to Aberdeen, was less than five miles down the harbor to the west. The *Aberdeen Herald* responded that "this will be news to Aberdeen union men and citizens generally, who know of no such feeling in regard to law abiding men, union or otherwise." The paper continued "that Aberdeen will not tolerate law breaking—whether done under the guise of unionism or any other—is as good an advertisement as this city desires. Gohl has not felt at home in Aberdeen since his piratical, and slugging methods would not be tolerated, nor do we believe the Gohl style of unionism will meet with very cordial reception in Hoquiam."

The newspaper's sentiment was echoed by T.T. Ford, agent for W.R. Grace and Company, a San Francisco shipping concern, who declared "that the present attitude of the Sailors' Union, as expressed through their representative, William Gohl" was "detrimental" to the company's interests, making it "impossible for the company to make prompt dispatch in loading and sending their vessels to sea from the harbor."

Anchored at the black tank buoy in the lower harbor and loaded with lumber from the Wilson Mill, Captain Ross of the schooner *Wilbert L. Smith* delivered a final message from W.R. Grace and Company that the organization would cease doing business in Grays Harbor and wouldn't be sending any more vessels to the port. Then the *Wilbert L. Smith* set sail for the return trip to San Francisco.

Gohl was sullying the reputation of Aberdeen and Grays Harbor all along the Pacific coast. He had damaged too much business and double-crossed too many accomplices. He had gone too far.

G ohl didn't see the trapdoor opening underneath him. With all the relationships and businesses he'd harmed, many in the town were working for his downfall. One of them was within his own gang.

A.W. Jakobbsen, one of Gohl's accomplices, had a "valuable rat terrier dog." By all accounts, Gohl disliked the dog. Two months after the fire that took out the Aberdeen Ship Chandlery Company and the Zelasko block, Jakobbsen's dog went missing. Not immediately concerned, Jakobbsen went about his business until someone called him on the phone to ask him whether he had found his dog.

Suspicious, he searched for the animal and ran into Gohl, who told him he had seen the dog aboard the steamer *Centralia* down at one of the mill docks. Convinced that a sailor was trying to steal his dog, he went to a judge and demanded a search warrant for the ship. Curiously, he was granted the warrant and searched the *Centralia* but found no sign of the animal. This took several hours, delaying the shipment of lumber. Gohl appeared again and insisted that the dog was onboard. The logistics of another search took another five hours, holding the steamer in port almost a day longer than scheduled.

Several days later, the body of Jakobbsen's dog was discovered floating in the Wishkah River under the SUP hall where Gohl kept his headquarters. The disappearance of the dog now appeared to be part of Gohl's tactic to delay the *Centralia* from leaving Grays Harbor. Jakobbsen saw the killing of the animal as nothing but spite. He was enraged.

Between the death of his dog and the "double crosses" he'd endured at Gohl's hand, Jakobbsen went to the authorities to inform on the man he once considered a friend. He told the police about the arson at the Alaska saloon, signing an affidavit swearing that Gohl admitted that he used the "infernal machine" to burn down the building. Two detectives were assigned to the case, but according to the *Aberdeen Herald*, they were taken off the case just as they were beginning to get results, suggesting that Gohl's influence still reached into the Aberdeen police department. And at one point, the town officially employed Deputy Sheriff Jacob Miller from Montesano as a "dog catcher"; his real job was to spy on Gohl. In short order, though, Miller turned and became Gohl's tool. He kept him informed of the moves of the mayor and the police. As for Jakobbsen, it's a wonder he didn't find himself face down in the harbor.

Ed Dolan, purportedly fed up with Gohl's activities, sold the Grand Saloon to Paddy McHugh. And Gohl, when drinking, started bragging to McHugh about his exploits. He told the new saloon owner about burning down half of Aberdeen, about the many enemies he had done away with. This may have been both braggadocio and threat.

McHugh held onto these stories, perhaps aware of how little had been done when Jakobbsen went to the police.

Then Ed Benn, a "young man" who had already been a city councilman and state representative, was elected mayor of Aberdeen. "Gregarious" Ed Benn was the grandson of the town founder, Sam Benn. Times were different and the lawlessness of Aberdeen had to be curbed. He pledged to get rid of the "undesirable element" of Aberdeen. During his campaign, he raised a "secret $10,000 war chest" to bring down Billy Gohl.

Benn appointed George Dean chief of police. Only twenty-seven, Dean was from Oregon and worked for the coast guard in Westport before moving to Aberdeen to manage a team of workers at the Slade Mill. For a time, he operated a grocery store with a man named Roy Sargent. Slender and personable, Dean had been the officer called to the scene of the fire that nearly burned down the mills.

Mayor Benn would find an unsuspected ally while "sojourning" at Green River Hot Springs near Seattle. Paddy McHugh was one of the other guests. According to Benn, the saloon owner sought him out and told him that he knew enough about Gohl to "send him to the gallows." When Benn returned to Aberdeen, he quietly instituted an investigation, using McHugh as a source of information. Newspapers of the time attribute the same exact quotes to two different men: Paddy McHugh and Billy Montana. The name Billy Montana never appears in any other context, so it was likely a codename given to McHugh during the investigation. But finding concrete evidence or people willing to inform on Gohl proved difficult. All Benn and Dean really had were accounts of Gohl's drunken confessions—not enough to ensure a successful prosecution.

When Gohl found out that Mayor Benn was working to bring him down, he ordered Hadberg to kill him. But Hadberg wouldn't get the chance.

Gohl bragged to McHugh about a trip to North Bay he took with Hadberg and Hoffman. West of Grays Harbor, North Bay is formed by a curved peninsula that opens in the Pacific Ocean where the lumber ships come and go. It's not clear what prompted the journey, but while they were there, they broke into the house of a Finnish family at Lone Tree Point in an area now known as Ocean Shores. The men raped the daughter. For good measure, they killed the family's cattle.

McHugh went directly to Chief Dean with the information. Dean took a boat trip to question the family, who said little. Afraid of what might happen, they refused to finger Gohl or his men. But Gohl heard about Dean's visit and went to the Grand Saloon, accusing McHugh of informing on him. The saloon owner was able to convince Gohl that either Hadberg or Hoffman had turned him in, maybe by reminding him of Jakobbsen's betrayal. Gohl told McHugh that he was going to kill them both.

A few days before Christmas, Gohl sent for Klingenberg and told him they had to go to Indian Creek to where Hadberg lived in a shack owned by Gohl on the north side of Grays Harbor. Klingenberg had lived in Grays Harbor for the past six years, a frequent companion of Gohl's in crime. Klingenberg was working on the anchored schooner *A.J. West*.

"We have to go," Gohl told him in the SUP office.

"Ain't that possible—ain't that possible to smooth that off in a little decent way?" Klingenberg pushed Gohl for another solution.

"No, there's no other way to do it. I'm staring into the penitentiary." Gohl told him about the incident on North Bay and gave Klingenberg a gun. The man shoved it in his pocket.

They left the union office, found Hoffman, and told him of a plan to steal a sloop down the bay, convincing him that they could take the sails or paint it and sell it. The three agreed to meet the next night to make the foray. One of them wouldn't return.

An empty tank has scuppered many a journey. It must have been infuriating to Gohl to go to his launch, *Patrol,* on the night of the expedition to Indian Creek and find he was short on gasoline. The stores were closed for the night. Maybe he thought he was lucky to find George Martell, a game warden, who gave him some fuel. But Martell remembered the date of the encounter because later that same night he arrested two men for illegal fishing in the lower harbor. Martell would place Gohl at the harbor that night.

Hoffman and Klingenberg joined him in the boat and the men set off for Indian Creek. A short distance below the Michigan Mill down the bay, Gohl stopped the launch and shot Hoffman with his Colt.

Hoffman begged for his life. "For God's sake, don't kill me, Billy. Don't kill me." He pleaded loudly enough that a man named Oswald Bell heard him from the shore near the Michigan Mill. Bell, "repairer of gasoline engines and automobiles," later claimed that he recognized the exhaust as that of the *Patrol.*

"You damn baby," Gohl said. "Why don't you die like a man?"

Gohl shot Hoffman three more times, then grabbed the man by the throat and put the revolver against his forehead, pulling the trigger. Several men heard the shots: John

Nikklovitch, the night watchman at the Lindstrom shipyards; a man named Ed Nelson whose launch had broken down near the scene of the shooting; and J.H. Hilts who called the police. All these men would be called as witnesses at Gohl's trial.

It was near 9 p.m. when Gohl and Klingenberg pushed Hoffman's body overboard tied to a stolen anchor. They continued on to Hadberg's cabin at the mouth of Indian Creek. Gohl ordered Klingenberg to shoot Hadberg the next day when he gave the signal. They left the *Patrol* on a spit just offshore in the low tide and trudged to the shack. A horseshoe and a pasteboard sign hung above the door. The sign read:

> Live every day so you can look every man in the eye and tell him to go to hell.
> —Indian Creek philosophy
> by Charles Hadberg

Photograph of Hadberg's cabin. 1910.

Terrified of Gohl, Klingenberg didn't sleep a wink that night at Hadberg's. Gohl didn't sleep either, concerned that Klingenberg would run.

When the men rose the next morning, they ate a hasty breakfast and started back to Gohl's launch in Hadberg's small rowboat. But the *Patrol's* engine wouldn't start despite repeated attempts. Gohl commanded them to row him back to town. They tethered the launch to the small rowboat. Before setting off, Gohl made the men move an anchor from the *Patrol* to the smaller craft. Klingenberg knew that Gohl would soon want him to kill Hadberg.

Gohl sat in the stern with Klingenberg rowing. Gohl signaled to Klingenberg, but the man didn't want to be a "coward" and shoot Hadberg in the back. Gohl made the men change places. Klingenberg withdrew his revolver and fired two shots into Hadberg's face. They threw the guns overboard, as well as a grip of tools taken from the launch, and cut the *Patrol* loose, which floated adrift until it beached a mile above the mouth to Indian Creek.

Gohl made Klingenberg bind Hadberg to the anchor and push him overboard. Klingenberg was shivering all over.

"If you did not take him, I would have done," Gohl said.

When they reached the shore at Aberdeen, Gohl had told "murder stories" the whole way back into town.

"I never could have done that, shot that man in the back," Klingenberg told Gohl. When Gohl said that Hoffman deserved it, Klingenberg responded, "I never could have done it if it hadn't been for you."

"We had to do this. I am staring right into the penitentiary," Gohl repeated.

In a move suggestive of Gohl's confidence in his ties to the police (or at least in his ability to bluff), he and Klingenberg ate a light lunch that day with Joe Searles, a police officer. Shaken as he was by the murders they'd committed just hours before, Klingenberg somehow got through the lunch without giving them away, but when they ran into Captain Smith of the *A.J. West* on the Heron Street bridge and he asked Klingenberg where he'd been, Gohl answered for them both. He said they'd been down the bay "on a little trip, but the launch broke down and we spent the night on the tide flats."

Klingenberg was a loose end and both men knew it. The next night Klingenberg went to the union office to pay his union dues. Gohl invited him to go hunting. While along the shore, Gohl asked him if he told anybody who he was going off with. When Klingenberg said he had, Gohl was quiet.

"I could see in the man that he was trying to put me out of business," Klingenberg said later.

Gohl abandoned his plan to kill Klingenberg and they headed back into town, meeting up with another cohort, Valdimar Nelson, at the Eagle saloon. They were "overanxious" to get Klingenberg alone. Gohl asked Klingenberg to head into the bay with him. Klingenberg declined. He had "some good idea in my head that Billy Gohl wanted to try to get me into a place where he could put lead in me."

Klingenberg went back to the *A.J. West*. Gohl followed him there, saying he had "some good thing on the string."

"Well," said Klingenberg, "what is it?"

"The crew from the schooner *Resolute* got paid off today and I am going down, and you are coming along. I am going to see an old mate, he cashed about $200 pay day, and if he are alone on board, I am going to have him."

"You better not. I have been in that schooner and the captain is always on board nights."

Despite Klingenberg's warning, they went to the *Resolute* that night, where Gohl had Klingenberg wait for him while he went aboard to shake down his "mate." All they walked away with was the ship's compass, but Klingenberg was nervous. Knowing full well that there had been several moments when Gohl could have killed him, he shipped off days later as a "donkeyman" on the *A.J. West* for Santa Rosalía, Mexico. Donkeymen tended the "donkey engine," the auxiliary steam engine used to winch cargo and sails that likely got its name from the original use of donkeys to power the winch. Klingenberg might have believed he was leaving Aberdeen for good.

Gohl went to the Grand Saloon and pulled McHugh aside.

"Well Paddy we landed those fellows last night, Hoffman was pretty tough we planted them in the mud with anchors for pillows. I guess they won't tell any more tales; I got wet to the waist when we threw Hadberg overboard, the water splashed all over me." He told McHugh that Klingenberg had helped him.

McHugh went to Mayor Benn. When Gohl was questioned about the disappearances of Hoffman and Hadberg, he said Hadberg had stolen money from him and left for Alaska in a fishing boat. Later, he adjusted the story, saying the man had accepted a job there as caretaker of a lighthouse making $75 per month. Dean and his men dredged more than ninety square miles of Grays Harbor with poles and grappling hooks without luck.

Perhaps Gohl thought he had gotten away with another murder, but he was reported to be a bit edgy. One Saturday morning, a couple of weeks after killing Hoffman, he had an altercation with kids who were "enjoying a little coasting" on Broadway Street hill outside his house. To stop them he scattered ashes on the walks. The boys swept off the ashes and continued sledding. He nailed slats across the walks to stop them. The boys pulled off the slats, infuriating Gohl. Gohl finally called the police, "whom, it is said, he is not at all times so anxious to see," according to a piece in a newspaper.

Then Charles Hadberg's body was discovered. On February 3, 1910, George Lightfoot and his brother were on their way home in a small boat along Indian Creek. It was low tide and Lightfoot saw a man's head in the water about eighteen inches below the surface. After rowing ashore and telling friends who lived close to the shore, he went into Aberdeen and told the police. Lightfoot said the head "pillowed on an anchor."

Chief Dean, Detective K.Y. Church, and Undertaker Randolph took a launch out to where Lightfoot said he found the body. The twenty-five-pound anchor holding down the body had been stolen from the Caldwell Brothers logging camp. The gun used to kill Hadberg was found thirty-five feet from the body. They took Hadberg to the morgue for autopsy. Chief Dean and Detective Church went to the union hall to arrest Billy Gohl.

W ith pistols drawn and taking no chances, Dean and Church came at Gohl from opposite directions.

"Keep your hands above the desk," Dean commanded. "Better come quietly."

This time, Gohl was held without bail. He claimed he was innocent, that Hadberg was his most intimate friend. He told the police that Hadberg's testimony years ago got him off when he was arrested for stealing automobile blankets and that he had no motive for killing the man. With the discovery of Hadberg's body, however, his story about the lighthouse job was clearly a lie. Gohl was upbeat, though, likely optimistic because of his previous success evading conviction. He waived his right to a preliminary hearing.

Defense Attorney Wilson Buttner took Gohl's case. Originally from Ohio, Buttner had come to Aberdeen a few years before. After setting up practice and house, his wife and daughter joined him. He was one of the attorneys who defended Charles Beasley for arson. Buttner remained on Gohl's case for one day. After hearing the evidence and talking to Gohl, the lawyer withdrew.

Word of Gohl's arrest spread quickly. There were gatherings and "some talk of mob violence." At 2 p.m. the day after he was arrested, a group of sailors and longshoremen went to the Aberdeen jail "pounding . . . and threatening to lynch

Gohl." Former intimates and victims of Gohl, perhaps now believing that their stories would be heard, began coming forward. People filed affidavits for crimes including "arson, robbery, burglary, cattle rustling, smuggling, poisoning, piracy and murder of numerous human beings and assorted animals."

The *Aberdeen Herald* would write,

> Wonder is expressed that the man should have been permitted to go on in his career for over six years without being overhauled by the authorities, especially as he had the habit of bragging about his crimes to his companions when in his cups.

The police moved Gohl to the county jail at Montesano, where he "passed a miserable night." Gohl was charged with the first-degree murder of Hadberg by Prosecuting Attorney William E. Campbell.

When Buttner withdrew, speculation abounded about Gohl's new lawyer. Based on the SUP's support of him in the past, people expected the union to step in and there were rumors of money to be spent on his defense. Delphin Delmas was mentioned. Delmas had defended Harry K. Thaw after the man killed architect Stanford White. Thaw was found not guilty by reason of insanity. The infamous love triangle between Thaw, White, and Evelyn Nesbit was made into a movie in 1955 starring a young Joan Collins as Nesbit, entitled *The Girl in the Red Velvet Swing*.

The other lawyer rumored to take Gohl's case was Clarence Darrow. Though the Scopes "Monkey" Trial and his defense of the "thrill killers" Leopold and Loeb were yet to come, Darrow had already achieved fame for his representation of unions and his activity in politics. He had also successfully defended notorious figures like William "Big Bill"

Haywood, Charles Moyer, and George Pettibone, Western Federation of Miners leaders who were charged with conspiring to murder the governor of Idaho.

But the rumors turned out to be just that. And the SUP was deafeningly silent, putting up no money to defend Billy Gohl. Even the SUP was done with him.

A.M. Abel, an Aberdeen lawyer, stepped in as Gohl's counsel, while the police dredged the waters near the mouth of Indian Creek for Hoffman's body. If his corpse wasn't found, the defense might contend that Hoffman killed Hadberg and then left the country. The dredging came up with a number of skeletons weighted down with anchors.

A bunch of sailors loyal to Gohl visited the morgue while Gohl was in Montesano. Saying that they knew Hadberg well, they claimed the body wasn't his. Detective Church, seeing through the sham, grabbed one of the sailors and made him confess that the day before he had positively identified Hadberg.

The union sailors didn't attend Hadberg's funeral even though the man had been a member in good standing. It was noted that this "token of respect is never omitted," suggesting that Gohl and Abel intended to build their defense on *corpus delicti*, literally "body of the crime"—that the man found in Indian Creek was not Hadberg. The sailors didn't go to Hadberg's funeral because, the defense could contend, Hadberg wasn't necessarily dead. No body, no crime.

Abel asked for a change of venue, arguing that Gohl couldn't get a fair trial in the county. Gohl continued to protest his innocence, claiming that he has actually helped police prevent crimes. The example he cited was a time he told them about cattle stealing.

The *Aberdeen Herald* received an anonymous letter signed "Jack" threatening to blow the newspaper plant up if the paper didn't stop printing articles about the Gohl case. The newspaper placed guards around the building. The paper continued to print articles about Gohl and the corruption in Chehalis County, arguing that it is "full time Chehalis county had a house cleaning" and contending that there had not been a clean election in ten years.

Newspapers across the country compared the case to that of Belle Gunness (called Hell's Belle, the Black Widow, and Lady Bluebeard) who may have killed and buried as many as forty people on her Indiana farm, "with the exception that the water and not the earth has been used for graves."

On February 14, Gohl was arraigned in the superior court in Montesano on the charge of the first-degree murder of Charles Hadberg. He pleaded not guilty and his trial was set for March 25. Anyone believing that Gohl's arrest would result in a quick peace in Aberdeen was in for a shock.

G ohl's arrest was "followed by a tremendous reign of terror." Investigators and witnesses received anonymous death threats. People on the streets were followed and "few had the temerity to venture forth after dark, and then only when guarded."

Photograph of Billy Gohl. 1910.

Soon after, Jacob Miller, the former deputy sheriff, and his wife disappeared. They had been living in a cabin on Laidlaw Island that belonged to Gohl. Police also determined that another man and woman that Gohl had threatened were missing.

Gohl believed he would go free and was presenting a respectable face to the newspapers. One reporter from out of state found him "a pleasant appearing fellow, highly educated, of quick wit and absolutely fearless. He is well read in law, and previous to his arrest said he intended to go to Germany to finish his law course. Since his incarceration Gohl has studied law almost continuously, and will, it is stated, take an active part in the conduct of his own defense."

Mayor Benn and Chief Dean enlisted the help of the famed Thiel Detective Service Company. The agency was formed by George H. Thiel, a former Civil War spy and Pinkerton employee. The Thiel Detective Service Company sent eight men to Aberdeen to work on the case, which cost the county $3,500. They gathered evidence of the murders of more than forty men. Chief Dean said he believed Gohl was the "greatest murderer of the age."

Accomplices were put under surveillance and former associates confessed, implicating Gohl in a plot to dynamite city hall and kill the mayor, chief of police, and several other prominent officials. The investigation determined that Gohl owned and maintained shacks in the woods on the shores of Grays Harbor at Indian Creek, Chenois Creek, Grass Creek, and South Bay for the purpose of "inveigling sailors and loggers who had money, and who were murdered and robbed in these lonely localities." The detectives from Thiel discovered a second trapdoor behind the cigar counter in Gohl's old shop that opened over the Wishkah River.

Theories circulated that a number of bodies would be found "near an old fish trap in Indian Creek." The search for Hoffman's body continued. The Aberdeen Lodge of Odd Fellows offered a $500 reward for its recovery.

A.M Abel's brother joined the defense team. W.H. Abel

was considered to be the "most successful criminal lawyer in Chehalis county." Because the defense was still not ready, the court date was moved from March 25 to May 2. Gohl told papers that he was broke and owed money and that his wife had to sell her jewelry to meet expenses since his arrest.

Then Gohl was nearly killed. Alexander Degoeff was assigned to him as a cellmate. The men had a longstanding grudge and Degoeff attacked him with a chair, beating him over the head. A deputy intervened, saving Gohl's life.

Things were about to get worse. John Klingenberg was coming back to Aberdeen.

A telegram had been sent weeks earlier to Captain H. Smith of the *A.J. West*. When the ship made port in Santa Rosalía, Mexico, the captain received the message to return to Grays Harbor with Klingenberg. He waited until the voyage was minutes from over to tell his anxious captive why he was being held and taken back. "You're wanted for the murder of Charles Hadberg and John Hoffman. Your friend Billy Gohl is cooling his heels in jail. See that launch—that's Dean coming out to arrest you."

"Thank God that's it," Klingenberg said. "I thought you were bringing me back to Billy . . . So he's in jail . . . I'm not a murderer. But I know who is. I'll tell everything . . . everything I know."

When the schooner came to anchor at the custom house in Aberdeen on April 4, Klingenberg was taken into custody. According to the captain, the man was an excellent sailor on the down voyage but was depressed on the trip north and relieved to be in the hands of the police.

Moved to the Grayport Hotel by Sheriff Payette before the transport to Montesano, he quickly made a full and notarized confession, "freely in broken language." Payette asked, "Where did you put the body of John Hoffman?"

"In the bay," he answered. "The man was shot through the

back three or four times. I could take any one to the place. If I hadn't shot Hadberg, he would have shot me, because I knew too much about this deal of Billy Gohl's."

Klingenberg took the authorities to where he and Gohl had dumped Hoffman's body. He was given the wheel of the boat and he steered to the spot near the mill where they had thrown the man overboard. Confessing as they looked for the body, he "wept like a child." He said that he had suffered for the crime and was ready to take the consequences. To a reporter, Klingenberg said, "I have not slept a peaceful night since the terrible crime was committed. I would lay in my bunk and when I fell asleep would be awakened by the face of our victims standing over me and in my ears would be ringing Hoffman's death words."

The area of the bay was dragged until dark, but no sign of Hoffman was found. They would continue the search the following day. Klingenberg was taken to Montesano to the jail where Gohl was housed. Both men were moved to solitary confinement. With additional leverage, the police pushed Gohl again for a confession. For two days, Bessie Gohl was refused permission to see her husband. Told of Klingenberg's confession, Gohl denied every bit of it. The interrogation was unsuccessful. But the pressure on Gohl increased.

Sailors had been returning to port over the past few weeks looking for the money that Gohl had supposedly been holding for them. They found their banker in jail and their accounts empty. Many turned to attorneys for help recovering their deposits.

During the investigation, over twenty men were implicated in his crimes over the years. According to police, "no effort will be spared to bring them to justice."

The dredging of the Chehalis brought up a piece of cloth identified as Hoffman's coat and, when it seemed grappling irons might have touched a body, divers from Hoquiam were brought in. Sheriff Payette even acquired a diving suit from the Lindstrom Shipbuilding Company and sent another diver down to make a careful examination of all the places where the drags had indicated a body might be. A body thought initially to be Hoffman's was found, but it was soon identified as Carl O. Carlson, yet another possible victim of Gohl's.

Gohl was in for another bit of bad news. After Klingenberg's confession, the Abel brothers withdrew from the case. The men claimed it was failure to pay the $10,000 needed for the defense, but most believe that the motive was the futility of the case. Gohl was "visibly affected when told of Abel's action."

The court appointed Arthur Cross of Aberdeen and J.A. Hutchinson of Montesano. Bessie Gohl was tireless in working to defend her husband. She sold four lots of land to raise money and traveled to Seattle to enlist the help of Will H. Morris, a former judge. Morris declined her request. Gohl had seen everyone but his wife desert him and his property sold off.

Meanwhile, Cross and Hutchinson worked to build their case against him, taking a boat to Indian Creek and Hadberg's shack. The trial date was coming up quickly.

9

Assembling a jury wasn't easy. It was tough to find men "who have not formed an opinion." The trial started at 10 a.m. on Monday, May 2, 1910. Over one thousand people showed up. Both Gohl and Klingenberg were brought into the courtroom in handcuffs to watch the jury selection. By now looking considerably different, Gohl sported a mustache and had taken to wearing glasses in jail. In a brown suit, "Gohl looked into the faces of the assemblage squarely and greeted his friends with a smile." He seemed to be "in fine spirits and chatted pleasantly with the newspaper men, although he maintained silence when asked questions regarding the case. He has taken on flesh since incarceration and appears little worried over the outcome." Klingenberg "looked the physical wreck."

Before the proceedings began, the defense entered an objection to the "entire venire" before the trial started, "laying the grounds for a reversal should Gohl be convicted." Judge Ben Sheeks denied the objection. Though this was Sheeks' first case as judge, he was no stranger to the courtroom. At sixty-seven, he had earned a reputation as an effective attorney. One of his cases was the defense of Brigham Young, the famous Mormon religious leader, against his nineteenth wife, Anna Eliza.

All the witnesses were excluded from the courtroom, with two exceptions. The defense agreed that A.C. Girard, a reporter and witness for the state, could remain if Gohl's wife could stay. When it was clear that his case wasn't going to be dismissed, she'd moved to Montesano to be near him.

Attorney W.E. Campbell was assisted by E.E. Boner, another one of the lawyers who defended Charles Beasley for the arson that Gohl committed a couple of years before. When the morning session was finished, only one juror had been accepted—a laborer at the Sunset shingle mill in Montesano.

Of the twenty-four jurors excused that day, seven admitted they had formed opinions of Gohl's innocence or guilt, seven opposed capital punishment, while the rest were excused for a variety of reasons. But the selection improved through the afternoon and the group of men who would decide Gohl's fate was growing.

When Gohl entered the court on the second day of the trial, Bessie was waiting with a bouquet of flowers. He put one of the flowers in his buttonhole and "toyed with the others as the examinations progressed." His wife was "in constant attendance" during the trial. In addition to the land she sold, she pawned her diamonds for funds to aid her husband's defense.

It took the entire second and most of the third day to secure a jury of twelve men. From the initial pool of 300 talesmen, 157 were examined. Judge Sheeks "was careful to give the defense no pegs upon which to hang an appeal and sustained their objections whenever possible." A high number were excused by the prosecution because of their opposition to the death penalty. The final panel, decided at 4:35 p.m. on day three, included only one person from Aberdeen and no sailors or ship workers. It consisted of six ranchers, two loggers, one engineer, the manager of the Aberdeen town dump, and a dentist.

Jury in Gohl case reading from left to right
Top row—H. W. Smithros, J. N. Simpson, J. E. Winston, O. C. Monk, O. L. Murray, W. L. Byng. Bottom row—Wm. Isaacs, W. J. Nealy, L. O. Stewart, O. W. Wood, J. H. Foster, Ned Harkett.

Photograph of the jury. 1910.

The county leased a completely furnished house for the jury for the entirety of the trial. Most believed the trial would end within a week. Gohl maintained a "demeanor of solid indifference," although he was "beginning to show the strain of the past three days." Concerned about violence or suicide, the judge refused Gohl's request for the use of a razor in his cell and secured the services of a city barber during his incarceration.

The state summoned eighty witnesses against Billy Gohl. Bessie Gohl wasted no time employing her husband's well-worn tactics to aid him if she could. One of the witnesses reported to Sheriff Payette that Gohl's wife met him on the street the night before and attempted to intimidate him. Bessie denied the charge.

Day four started with the prosecution's opening statement. Attorney Campbell contended that "the state will prove that William Gohl on the morning of December 22, 1909, did command one John Klingenberg to fire the fatal shots which killed Charles Hadberg, and that Gohl premeditated and designed to kill said Hadberg. The state will also show that Gohl gave Klingenberg the gun with which he killed Hadberg; that the gun was the property of William Gohl; also that the Colts automatic revolver found near Hadberg's body belonged to Gohl and was thrown overboard after Hadberg's body had been anchored in the stream."

When the murder allegedly occurred was in contention. The defense had expected and hoped for the prosecution to put the date of the killing as December 23. Gohl had a strong alibi for the night. The opening statement was a blow to Gohl's defense.

While Campbell spoke, Gohl "sat attentively watching Campbell, and at times spoke to his attorneys and had them make notes of Campbell's statements." The prosecutor declared that

> the state would also prove that Gohl fired the shots that killed John Hoffman and that his "death cries" were heard by people on shore. Objecting to the mention of Hoffman, the defense demanded that the jury be discharged. Judge Sheeks instructed Campbell not to mention Hoffman's name again in his opening statement.

The first witness was George L. Lightfoot who found Hadberg's body in Indian Creek. His testimony was corroborated by his brother, William Lightfoot, and another man, George Marshall. Seven witnesses were questioned.

Later that day, a gruesome exhibit was introduced into evidence. A piece of human flesh, with a tattoo of a rose pierced by a dagger with the initials "H.H." beneath. The embalmed section had been cut from Hadberg's corpse. The defense argued that Hadberg's initials were "C.H.," but Hadberg's given name was Henry. The anchor used to weight down the body was brought into the courtroom, and the blood-smeared clothing of the dead man was spread on the floor near the defendant's chair. Gohl "gazed at these articles as though fascinated."

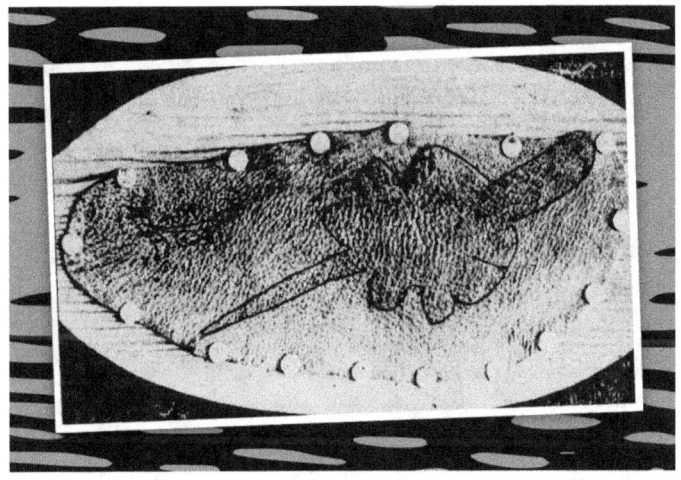

Photograph of piece of Hadberg's skin showing tattoo marks. 1910.

Hadberg's body was positively identified by "numerous witnesses." Emil Olson, a shipmate of the victim on the schooner *F.M. Slade*, testified that he had seen the tattoo "on many occasions, when his shipmate had rolled up his sleeves to wash himself, or while at work." Oswald Bell, one of the men who had heard Hoffman's "death cries," owned a repair business in Aberdeen and recognized the tattoo as well because Hadberg "spent many hours" in his shop. Another of the defense tactics had been destroyed. "No effort was made to resist identification."

Over the following days, Campbell and the prosecution methodically and exhaustively built their case. They called witnesses to connect Gohl with the ownership of the launch *Patrol* and established Gohl's boat trip as the night of Hoffman's murder through testimony from the game warden

George Martell. Oswald Bell, J.H. Hilts, and the night watchman of the Lindstrom shipyards, John Nikklovitch, all testified to hearing a man being killed on the bay.

The defense objected repeatedly to the discussion of Hoffman's murder, particularly since the man's body had yet to be found. Some objections were sustained and some denied. The jury was finally excused from the courtroom so that attorneys could discuss whether discussion of Hoffman was allowed. The state contended that "while it is not general rule to introduce evidence of a crime with which the defendant is connected prior to the commission of the crime for which he is being tried, yet there were many cases in which the rule has been excepted." Campbell's intention was to use Hoffman's murder as the motive for Klingenberg's killing of Hadberg. Judge Ben Sheeks took the matter under advisement.

The moment that many had been waiting for had arrived. John Klingenberg was called to the stand.

10

K lingenberg was a husk of his former self. He could see Billy Gohl from the witness stand. The man regarded the young Dane coolly, his blue eyes boring into him, as Klingenberg told the story of meeting up with Gohl and heading out with Hoffman in the *Patrol*. In his accented English, he described the murder of Hoffman and the man begging for his life. And that Gohl said the man "died like a baby."

When he "came to his shooting of Hadberg at the alleged command of Gohl, Klingenberg's voice broke and tears welled up in his eyes." One newspaper reporter wrote that his tears were

> unquestionably genuine. His testimony made a decided impression. He did not seek once to shield himself, yet there was no bravado apparent. He painted himself in dark colors, yet his story had the sound of truth. . . . Though the attorneys for the defense plied Klingenberg searchingly with questions during the examination, he answered all without hesitation and not once could he be tripped.

In a surprising turn, Klingenberg also claimed that Gohl told him that if he hadn't shot Hadberg, his wife, Bessie, would have.

The next day Paddy McHugh, a.k.a. "Billy Montana," would be the first witness called to the stand. By the time of the trial, McHugh had sold the Grand Saloon and purchased the Baldwin Hotel in Hoquiam. His ties to the business community in both towns became apparent. Before going to Mayor Benn, he had approached the Royal Arch Masonic Chapter, to which many of the businessmen of Aberdeen belonged. It's likely that Benn's war chest for the apprehension of Gohl was substantially funded by the Royal Arch. The damage to the businesses of Grays Harbor and the safety of the community had driven the businessmen to organize on their own.

McHugh recounted Gohl's confession of the killing of the two men and the involvement of Klingenberg. He told the jury of Gohl's brag that he "planted them in the mud with anchors for pillows." The man's testimony was another blow to the defense.

The defense attempted to impugn McHugh's credibility, claiming the saloon owner demanded $7,000 from Gohl not to testify. McHugh "emphatically denied" this. The threat to his character wasn't the only threat McHugh endured, though. After testifying against Gohl, he began to receive threats of violence. Bessie Gohl "told McHugh that he would die as the result of the stand he took against her husband." And later that year, police would foil a plot to dynamite McHugh's recently acquired property, the Baldwin Hotel.

One person who showed marked improvement was Klingenberg, who, after his confession, was "in the best of spirits." He posed for a photographer and said he wanted to send a picture to his aged mother and father, who resided in Copenhagen, where he was born. He would never see his home again.

Several more witnesses were examined, but the defense, recognizing the inevitability of a guilty verdict, asked less than a half a dozen questions. Over the past few days, Gohl was "a nervous wreck in his cell at night." Growing "more excited and restless every day," his actions were described as "mechanical" and "he hardly moved his gaze from the witnesses." Both he and Bessie showed signs of strain.

But Campbell was taking no chances. Calling William Griggs, a former hardware dealer in Aberdeen, he connected Gohl to the 38-caliber revolver found in the tide flat mud close to Hadberg's body. The number on the weapon was sent to the factory and traced by duplicate invoice to Grigg's hardware store. Griggs produced the invoice that corresponded to the gun found in the mud and testified that he had sold the weapon to Gohl.

When the superior court adjourned a 4 p.m. on day six of the trial, the result was, according to the *Aberdeen Herald*, "a tightening of the coils of the law about William Gohl to an extent his appearance seems to indicate he fully realizes. Thus far the case against the accused murderer shows that great care has been taken in marshaling the evidence and that nothing is being left to chance."

The following day, the day of closing arguments, was eventful.

○━○━○

I n the morning, two fishermen hooked a body by the mouth and brought it to the surface. Before the men could pull the body into the boat, the flesh gave way. The lost body was believed to be John Hoffman's. Detective Church and Undertaker Randolph were wired at Montesano and returned to Aberdeen on the noon train. They searched the bottom of the river but were unable to find the body.

While Church and Randolph were dragging the river, a human head was found on a beach at Laidlaw Island. The head had been severed from the body "by artificial means, with the flesh still clinging in shreds to the skull." The head was believed to be that of Gus Miller, a former friend of Gohl's, who disappeared after an argument with the man.

In Montesano, H.C. Lundberg, the man filling in for Gohl as agent for the SUP, was in the courtroom when he wasn't supposed to be. Judge Sheeks ordered him out and, in leaving, Lundberg tossed a revolver out the window to another man. In the corridor, he "accosted" Captain Smith of the *A.J. West*, saying "most of the witnesses for the state have told nothing but lies." When Smith challenged the man about threatening witnesses, Lundberg swung at the captain. During a fight that last several minutes, Smith gave Lundberg "a terrible thrashing." Lundberg was arrested and jailed. Sheeks and Smith had likely foiled a plot by Gohl's confederates.

Inside the courtroom, the state was completing its case against Billy Gohl. It was soon the defense's turn.

But in a shocking move, Hutchinson and Cross ended their defense only an hour and twenty minutes after calling the first witness. The attorneys had originally intended to call at least thirty witnesses but had only three take the stand. The testimony of the witnesses for the prosecution was so "damning" that the defense attorneys feared that cross examination would expose more crimes of "this gang of murderous pilfering pirates." One of the last-ditch efforts of the defense was to request dismissal of the case because the word "premeditated" had been spelled incorrectly in official documents. The desperate request was overruled by the court.

On the day of final arguments, an exceptionally large crowd came to Montesano. The audience was hoping to hear Billy Gohl make a plea on his own behalf. They would be disappointed.

At 10 a.m., Special Assistant Prosecuting Attorney Boner began carefully going over the presented evidence, "handling the grewsome exhibits one at a time." He told the jury that Hadberg's killing "was one of the most atrocious and cold blooded murders in the history of the state of Washington." Many must have considered the full catalog of Gohl's killings when Boner spoke, imagining the untold numbers of men who had been shot, poisoned, and drowned by Gohl's hand.

Gohl appeared unmoved during arguments and paid strict attention to every word. He "colored at times" when he was called a "cowardly low down cur" or when Boner made particular mention of the murder.

Bessie Gohl, foreseeing her husband's fate, broke down during the arguments and openly wept. Newspaper accounts had mentioned her remarkable "resolve" throughout the trial.

Associate Counsel J.A. Hutchinson started the arguments for the defense, warning the jury against accepting circumstantial evidence and suggesting that Gohl was the victim of a plot. A.E. Cross took over, casting doubt on the reliability of Klingenberg's confession and insisting there was no proof that Hoffman was dead or that the body recovered was that of Hadberg.

Judge Sheeks' instructions to the jury lasted only twelve minutes. He told them that "although the revolver was held in the hands of one other than William Gohl, that if the jury thought the defendant was present and aided, commanded and directed the shooting of the deceased that the jury must bring in a verdict of murder in the first degree."

When the jury left the courtroom to deliberate, the prosecution filed charges for Hoffman's murder in order to hold Gohl in the event of the man's acquittal. The charges wouldn't be pressed if Gohl was convicted of killing Hadberg.

As Gohl was led back to his cell, he told Bessie to get a lawyer for Lauritz "the Weasel" Jentzen, who was being held in Elma on the charge of poisoning Jakobbsen's dog. He also sent for Father Gribben, the Catholic priest of Aberdeen, spending some time quietly with the clergyman. When Father Gribben went to his cell unbidden later that day, Gohl said, "I shook hands with you this morning. That's all I want of you. You can't get any confession out of me.'"

He didn't sleep that night.

11

The jury was out for nearly ten hours and returned for instructions only once, to ask whether premeditation was essential to second-degree murder. The first ballot was 10–2 guilty. The sticking point for two members of the jury was the likelihood of the death penalty if they returned a guilty verdict for murder in the first degree. Seven ballots were taken before they agreed. The jury was able to come to a unanimous decision through the compromise that a recommendation for clemency be included in its verdict.

At 12:45 p.m. on May 12, 1910, Gohl was found guilty for the first-degree murder of Charles Hadberg. Gohl didn't flinch as the foreman, L.O. Steward, delivered the jury's decision. When asked if he had anything to say, Gohl "cursed the jury for its decision and said he was prepared to appeal the case." Bessie visited her husband in his cell afterward and told him, "I will stick with you to the end, Billy." She appeared "heartbroken," but immediately went to work raising money for an appeal.

Gohl complained that he hadn't gotten a fair trial, that his attorneys hadn't had time to prepare his case, and that witnesses who would have provided him with an alibi were turned away from the courthouse.

Sheeks delayed sentencing for two days to give the defense time to file for a new trial or appeal. "Learned attorneys" who followed the case closely believed that Judge Sheeks conducted the case so well that there was nothing for the defense to hang an appeal on.

The *Aberdeen Herald* again criticized the job the authorities had done and the cost of that incompetence or willful negligence. One article attacked the cost of bringing Gohl to justice, arguing that it should have been done earlier and less expensively. The expenses of the Thiel agency, the special venire of three hundred jurors, prosecutors, the hunt for Hoffman's body, special deputies, bailiffs, the cost of keeping witnesses for three months, and boarding the jury brought the cost of the trial to over $20,000—what would be $500,000 today.

On the heels of the Gohl trial, the newspaper demanded investigations into corruption.

> Since the elections of four years ago, this county has been filled with rumors of suspected illegal practices in county offices, rumors of crooked elections returns, unlawful dealing with the county funds, unsavory stories over the new court house, and in fact with nearly all the offices in the court house, that, in justice to the public and those accused should have been run down long ago and either proved or the accused publicly exonerated.

Judge Sheeks carefully considered the recommendations of the jury. The defense filed three motions: for an acquittal despite the verdict, an arrest of judgment, and an appeal for a new trial. Sheeks overruled them all and passed his sentence: life in prison. After two days of expecting the death penalty, both Billy and Bessie Gohl smiled with relief and "took the ruling in a calm, matter-of-fact way."

Sheeks knew he had to explain his leniency. He wrote, "Three matters in connection with the case may be thought of weight in inducing the court to inflict the lesser degree of punishment." First, unusual as it was, Sheeks admitted that the large number of jurors who'd been disqualified because they didn't believe in capital punishment had "continually recurred to the mind of the court." Second, he took into account the recommendation of leniency by the convicting jury. And finally, he felt that Klingenberg's testimony had to be viewed with "great caution" as it was in the man's interest to put as much of the blame for the death of Hadberg on Gohl as possible. There was enough doubt in Sheeks' mind to forestall the death penalty.

Billy Gohl was sentenced to life imprisonment at the state penitentiary in Walla Walla, Washington. On June 14, he was escorted by "Traveling Guard" Joseph Graham to prison to begin his sentence. Bessie Gohl moved to Walla Walla to be near him.

Before the summer was out, another body was discovered along the banks of Indian Creek. The flesh was gone from the bones, leaving a bare skeleton, and the skull had been mashed in as if by a blunt instrument. Another member of the "floater fleet." Bodies would be found for years to come.

Campbell charged John Klingenberg with the second-degree murder of Hadberg, citing a lack of premeditation for not charging him in the first degree. When Klingenberg told the story of the murders in his trial, it was consistent with the tale he told in Gohl's trial. The jury took less than three hours to find him guilty. He was sentenced to twenty-five years in Walla Walla and was taken to prison by the same traveling guard on the night of November 9 to serve his sentence alongside his one-time partner in crime Billy Gohl. Both men were denied new trials.

Gohl's ambitions to study law never materialized. The next spring the traveling guard that took him to Walla Walla reported that Gohl was learning the trade of plumber, hoping for a pardon which never came.

George Dean, chief of police and the man credited with the arrest of Gohl, resigned to enter the billiard and cigar business. With his brother, he purchased the Fan Cigar and Billiard Room on Heron Street. His brother, Al Dean, played baseball for two seasons in the Midwest before returning to Aberdeen to go into business with George.

Aberdeen was fast becoming a leader in shipping and lumber. With the advent of the First World War, the demand for ships and wood skyrocketed, and the town's shipyards duly expanded. When the U.S. Shipping Board put out a call for the nation's shipyards to build vessels in record time, the Grays Harbor Motorship Yard set the record for fastest ship construction with the launch of the four-thousand-ton *Aberdeen*. They built it in seventeen days. An official of the company, backed up by a U.S. inspector, testified to the speed of construction: "Laying of keel, 10 seconds; assembling, building erecting and shoring 73 square frames, 29 hours, 26 minutes; ceiling, 151 hours; planking 228 hours." And in 1924, Aberdeen shipped its one-billionth board foot of timber and became known, at least for a while before the Great Depression pulled the whole industry down, as the "Lumber Capital of the World."

The *Aberdeen Herald* wrote that Aberdeen was "not a backwoods camp, but a modern, civilized city. The days of the Gohls have gone by, as those who attempt to revive them will learn to their cost." During those days, Gohl killed at least 40 men and possibly as many as 150, more than Ted Bundy, John Wayne Gacy, or Jeffrey Dahmer.

In March 1912, Bessie Gohl was granted a divorce on the grounds that her husband was a convict. The last person to stand by Billy Gohl finally left him. A few months later, the

Grand Saloon burned down, taking Gohl's old SUP office with it—one fire he did not set.

Billy Gohl would not die until May 3, 1927, after years of exhibiting increasingly erratic behavior. He had contracted syphilis at some point in his checkered career and died from its complications alone in a hospital bed in the Eastern State Hospital at Medical Lake in Spokane County, still officially an inmate of Walla Walla state prison.

A Word From C.J. March

Thank you for reading *Ghoul of Grays Harbor*. If you have thoughts on this book or suggestions for other true crime accounts, please let us know at cjmarch@deadtruecrime.com. We love hearing from readers. You're why we write.

Sign up for our mailing list to learn about new Dead True Crime books and to read and listen to a free, exclusive story: www.deadtruecrime.com/ebook.

If you're interested in reading more Billy Gohl, check out the bibliography at the end of the book.

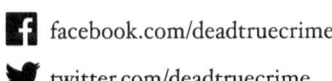

facebook.com/deadtruecrime

twitter.com/deadtruecrime

Other Dead True Crime Books

Sacrificial Axe
Voodoo Cult Slayings in the Deep South

The "Axe-man" came in the night. No one heard him come. No locks could keep him out. In the morning, whole families lay slaughtered in their beds, a riot of blood corrupting the room. Town by town, terror gripped the black communities of Louisiana and East Texas, as men, women, and children fell to the killer's ax. The police were powerless to stop it. Was it simply a homicidal maniac on the loose, or was a deeper evil afoot? Could one person perpetrate over forty atrocities? Was the serial killer even a man? People whispered voodoo, and white newspapers in the Jim Crow era South fanned the hysteria. As the police slowly unraveled the mystery, they were stunned by the bizarre truth of the "Axe-man."

Get Sacrificial Axe

Poison Widow
Arsenic Murders in the Jazz Age

First, she predicts your death. Then, you die. Usually, writhing in pain. Is she a fortune teller, or something much, much darker? Nobody tells the police, not for a long time, because, well, nobody in Chicago's Little Warsaw wants to cross Tillie Klimek. The body count racks up as Jazz Age Chicago's most notorious female poisoner takes down husband after husband, and some other relatives while she's at it. Few, it seems, can resist Tillie's cooking. But is this Mrs. Bluebeard working alone? Or is she part of a bigger, more diabolical "poison trust"? And can Chicago's Finest get to her before her latest husband, already mortally ill, dies? *Poison Widow* is a true-crime aficionado's feast, arsenic-laced and stuffed with tasty noir morsels.

Get Poison Widow

Murderer's Gulch

Carnage in the Catskills

Don't turn your back on her. Don't even blink. She may be crazy, but Lizzie Halliday is strong, she moves fast, and she's a stone cold killer. When famed journalist Nellie Bly interviews the woman the New York Times called "The Worst Woman on Earth," she has no idea how easy it would be for Lizzie Halliday to make Bly her next victim. In the peaceful Catskills in upstate New York, Halliday dispatches husbands, neighbors and peddlers by fire, poisoning and gunshot. The bloody death count at the Halliday farm earns it the name, "Murderer's Gulch." But even after she's arrested and committed to an insane asylum, Lizzie Halliday will kill again.

Get Murderer's Gulch

Killer Genius
The Bizarre Case of the Homicidal Scholar

He's a doctor whose patients have a way of dying; a lawyer, who uses his skills to squirm out of criminal convictions. He's a scholar, but other scholars have no idea what he's talking about. He's a family man, but one day, his wife and baby disappear forever. Only two things are clear: Edward Rulloff is a mystery, and everywhere he goes, death and destruction follow. While the criminal justice system has its hands full trying to keep and convict Edward Rulloff, the world will argue whether he's a genius, a scam artist or a madman. Even Mark Twain has an opinion.

Get Killer Genius

Coming Soon

Exit Row
Mass Murder in the Canadian Sky

A clear day. An experienced pilot. A routine flight. An obsessive love-triangle. What could go wrong? When a mysterious package follows J. Albert Guay's wife on board Flight 108, calamity is just a few ticks of the clock away. How far will a man go for his adulterous passion?

Cannibal Cowboy
Murder and Man-Eating on the American Frontier

Gold Rush and gunfights, scalping and saloons, the Old West had a reputation to uphold. But even the rough and tumble frontier wasn't ready for the likes of the Kentucky Cannibal. Mountain man and gunfighter Boone Helm would do anything to survive, right down to eating his enemies. Or his friends.

Blood Trade
Slaughter on the Underground Railroad

Nothing could be worse than slavery. Unless it was Patty Cannon hunting you down. A gang of thugs at her command, the woman infamous for her blood-thirst and brutality murdered free blacks and fugitive slaves alike for decades. Working her illegal slave trade in what became known as the Reverse Underground Railroad, Cannon's grisly tactics still have the power to chill centuries later.

About the Author

C.J. March is the alter ego of three true crime enthusiasts who wanted to write the kind of juicy noir histories they like to read. Between them they have: 2 MFAs, 3 arrests, 4 folk albums, 73 years of therapy, 1 stint working for "the artist formerly known as" which ended in a shoving match, 40 years of writing, 30 years of design, 3 dogs, and 1 overnight in a cell with a murderer.

Bibliography

"150 Corpses Rise From The Depths To Face Mr. Gohl." Oregon Daily Journal, *March 20, 1910.*

"Aberdeen Police Capture Greatest Murderer Of Age." Spokane (WA) Press, *February 3, 1910.*

"Accused Of Double Murder." Aberdeen (WA) Herald, *February 3, 1910.*

"After Captain Henningsen." Aberdeen (WA) Herald, *November 2, 1908.*

"Agent Assaults Witness." Aberdeen (WA) Herald, *May 12, 1910.*

"Agent of Union Is Held For Trial." Evening Statesman *(Walla Walla, WA), August 28, 1906.*

"Another Murder Case Near Close, Police Search." Eugene (OR) Guard, *May 9, 1910.*

"Arrest Engineer For Slaying of Two." Oakland (CA) Tribune, *April 5, 1910.*

"Arrest To Clear Forty Tragedies." Chicago Daily Tribune, *February 4, 1910.*

Asbury, Herbert. The Barbary Coast: An Informal History of the San Francisco Underworld. *Philadelphia, PA: Basic Books, 2008. First published 1933.*

"Ask Investigation of Wreck of the Falk." Statesman Journal *(Salem, Oregon), April 9, 1909.*

"Body of John Hoffman Found." Aberdeen (WA) Herald, *May 9, 1910.*

"Body Undiscovered." Aberdeen (WA) Herald, *February 10, 1910.*

"Carelessness Alleged." Aberdeen (WA) Herald, *April 15, 1909.*

"City and Country." Washington Standard, *March 18, 1910.*

"Clew To Body Of Victim Is Found." San Francisco Call, *April 8, 1910.*

"Coast News Notes." San Francisco Examiner, *November 4, 1909.*

"Coast Shipping News." San Francisco Call, *August 24, 1906.*

"Coast Shipping News." San Francisco Call, *August 31, 1906.*

"Comrade Relates How Slayer Gohl 'Sent 2 To Hell.'" Oregon Daily Journal, *May 8, 1910.*

"Confesses Crime." Los Angeles Times, *April 6, 1910.*

"Confesses To Murder Of Chas. Haderg." Eugene (OR) Guard, *April 6, 1910.*

"Convicted Murderer Curses The Jury." Billings (MT) Gazette, *May 13, 1910.*

"Convicted Slayer's Wife Trying To Raise Fund For Expense Of Court Appeal." Tacoma (WA) Times, *May 14, 1910.*

"Cotterill For President." Spokane (WA) Press, *March 9, 1907.*

"Court Appoints Attorneys When Gohl Is Deserted." Oregon Daily Journal, *April 24, 1910.*

Davidson, Lance, S. *"Shanghaied! The Systematic Kidnapping of Sailors in Early San Francisco."* California History *64, no. 1 (Winter, 1985).*

"Deny That Either Delmas Or Darrow Are Retained." Evening Statesman *(Walla Walla, WA), February 8, 1910.*

"Dog Responsible For Arrest And Trial Of Slayer." Oregon Daily Journal, *May 8, 1910.*

"'Donkey Man' Under Suspicion." Spokane (WA) Press, *April 5, 1910*.

"Engineer Arrested In Murder Mystery." San Francisco Call, *April 6, 1910*.

"Fail to Find Hoffman's Body." Aberdeen (WA) Herald, *April 11, 1910*.

"Fate of Gohl, Alleged Slayer, Going To Jury." Los Angeles Herald, *May 11, 1910*.

"Fight For Gohl's Life Starts At Montesano, WN." Oregon Daily Journal, *May 5, 1910*.

"Find Human Head On Beach." Tacoma (WA) Times, *May 10, 1910*.

"Get Eleven Men." Statesman Journal *(Salem, Oregon), May 4, 1910*.

"Gohl Butts In." Aberdeen (WA) Herald, *January 10, 1910*.

"Gohl Case To Finish Today." Statesman Journal (Salem, Oregon), *May 11, 1910*.

"Gohl Denies Confession." Spokane (WA) Press, *April 14, 1910*.

"Gohl Enters Plea of Not Guilty." Oregon Daily Journal, *February 15, 1910*.

"Gohl Expects New Trial." San Francisco Examiner, *June 15, 1910*.

"Gohl Guilty Of Murder In First Degree." Spokane Press, *May 12, 1910*.

"Gohl, Leader of Gang of Murderers." Aberdeen (WA) Herald, *April 7, 1910*.

"Gohl Murder Trial." Tacoma (WA) Times, *May 3, 1910*.

"Gohl Murder Trial On." Topeka (KS) State Journal, *May 2, 1910*.

"Gohl On Trial For His Life." Statesman Journal *(Salem, Oregon), May 3, 1910*.

"Gohl Pleads Not Guilty." Los Angeles Herald,
    February 15, 1910.

"Gohl's Lawyer Argues Long To Jurymen." Eugene
    (OR) Guard, *May 11, 1910.*

"Gohl's Past Life Is Resurrected." East Oregonian
    (Pendleton, OR), February 5, 1910.

"Gohl's Wife Wants Funds For Appeal." San
    Francisco Call, *May 14, 1910.*

"Grew Rich By Robbery And Murder." Capital
    Journal *(Salem, Oregon), April 29, 1910.*

"Grewsome Exhibits At Murder Trial." The
    Anaconda (MT) Standard, *May 6, 1910.*

Hughes, John C., and Ryan Teague Beckwith, eds. On
    the Harbor: From Black Friday to Nirvana.
    Las Vegas, NV: Stephens Press,, 2005.

"Is Charged With A Second Murder." Vancouver
    (BC) Daily World, *May 11, 1910.*

*"Items of Interest From Our State: Gohl To Make
    Appeal."* Newport (WA) Miner, *May 19, 1910.*

"Jury Finds Gohl Is Guilty." Tacoma *(WA) Times,*
    May 12, 1910.

"Klingenberg On Stand Against Murder Master."
    Oregon Daily Journal, *May 6, 1910.*

"Law Coils Tighten on Accused Murderer,"
    Aberdeen (WA) Herald, *May 9, 1910.*

"Lawyer Deserts Gohl." Aberdeen (WA) Herald,
    April 25, 1910.

*Lewarne, Charles Pierce. "The Aberdeen,
    Washington, Free Speech Fight of 1911–1912."*
    Pacific Northwest Quarterly *66, no 1
    (January 1975).*

*"Life Imprisonment." Aberdeen (WA) Herald, May
    26, 1910.*

"Lodge Offers $500 For Hoffman's Body." Aberdeen
(WA) Herald, *March 14, 1910.*

"May Lynch Suspect." Tacoma (WA) Times,
February 4, 1910.

Morgan, Murray. The Last Wilderness. *Seattle:
University of Washington Press, 1955.*

"Montesano Gossip." Aberdeen (WA) Herald,
February 14, 1910.

*"Montesano Murder Trial." Spokane (WA) Press,
May 4, 1910.*

*"More Evidence Against Gohl." Los Angeles Times,
February 6, 1910.*

"Move Gohl To Escape A Mob." Los Angeles
Times, *February 5, 1910.*

"Movements Of Vessels In All Parts Of World." San
Francisco Call, *April 28, 1910.*

"Mrs. Gohl Moves To Montesano." Statesman
Journal *(Salem,* Oregon), *May 18, 1910.*

*"Mrs. Gohl Will Stick To Husband Who Has Been
Found Murderer."* Tacoma (WA) Times, *May
12, 1910.*

"Murder Case Up May 2." Newport (WA) Miner,
March 24, 1910.

*"Murder Charged." Tacoma (WA) Times, February 3,
1910.*

"Murder, First Degree, Charge Against Gohl."
Oregon Daily Journal, *February 12, 1910.*

"Murder Will Out." Ogden (UT) Standard, *May 2,
1910.*

"Murderer Confesses Implicating Wm. Gohl."
Roseburg (OR) Review, *April 6, 1910.*

"Must Pay His Fine." Los Angeles Times, *August
4, 1907.*

"Only 3 Witnesses For Gohl Defense." East Oregonian *(Pendleton, OR), May 10, 1910.*

"Plot Is Laid To Kill Officials At Aberdeen." San Francisco Examiner, *February 14, 1910.*

"Retribution For the Mysterious Murders of Sailors is at Hand." Charlotte (NC) News, *April 6, 1910.*

"Sailors Taken From Ship." San Francisco Call, *August 23, 1906.*

"Says He Can Prove Innocence of Deed." Anaconda (MT) Standard, *February 21, 1910.*

"Shipping Mystery Baffles Police." San Francisco Call, *August 21, 1906.*

"Sixty Murders Charged To Man." Evening Kansan-Republican *(Newton, Kansas), April 30, 1910.*

"Slayer Of Haderg Tells Story Of Deed." Newport (WA) Miner, *May 12, 1910.*

"Suspected Of Many Crimes." Aberdeen (WA) Herald, *February 7, 1910.*

"Tales of the Town Tersely Told." Aberdeen (WA) Herald, *November 8, 1906.*

"Tales of the Town Tersely Told." Aberdeen (WA) Herald, *July 8, 1907.*

"Tales of the Town Tersely Told." Aberdeen (WA) Herald, *April 16, 1908.*

"Their Trade Was Murder, Wholesale." Leavenworth *(WA) Echo, April 8, 1910.*

"To Call Grand Jury." Aberdeen (WA) Herald, *May 2, 1910.*

"Sailors' Agent Held For Murder." Newport (WA) Miner, *February 10, 1910.*

"Second Murder Charge Against WM. Gohl Is Filed." Oregon Daily Journal, *May 10, 1910.*

"The Sailors' Union elected the following:" San Francisco Call, *January 16, 1904.*

"Trial of Aberdeen Slayer Begins Monday." San Francisco Call, *April 29, 1910.*

"Twelve Men to Try Wm. Gohl Are Chosen." Aberdeen (WA) Herald, *May 5, 1910.*

"Vale, William Gohl." Aberdeen (WA) Herald, *June 24, 1909.*

Van Syckle, Edwin. The River Pioneers: Early Days on Grays Harbor. *Seattle: Pacific Search Press, 1982.*

Van Syckle, Edwin. they tried to cut it all. *Seattle: Pacific Search Press, 1980.*

"Venire Is Drawn In WM. Gohl Case." Oregon Daily Journal, *April 10, 1910.*

"WM. Gohl May Appeal Case." Aberdeen (WA) Herald, *May 16, 1910.*

"William Gohl At Walla Walla." Oregon Daily Journal, *June 14, 1910.*

"William Gohl Found Guilty." Morning Register *(Eugene, Oregon), May 12, 1910.*

"William Gohl on Trial for Murder." Aberdeen (WA) Herald, *May 2, 1910.*

"William Gohl On Trial Monday." Oregon Daily Journal, *May 1, 1910.*

"William Gohl's Trial Begins At Montesano, WN." Oregon Daily Journal, *May 2, 1910.*

"Witnesses Tell Story of Gohl's Alleged Crime." Oregon Daily Journal, *May 7, 1910.*

Image Credits

CHAPTER 1

Photograph of Billy Gohl. Courtesy Aberdeen Herald, *April 11, 1910.*

CHAPTER 2

Photograph of Aberdeen. Early 1900s. Courtesy JonesPhotoCollection.com, Jones Photo Historical Collection.

Billy and Bessie's marriage certificate. 1905. Courtesy Findagrave.com, Find A Grave.

CHAPTER 3

Chehalis River. 1900s. Courtesy JonesPhotoCollection.com, Jones Photo Historical Collection.

CHAPTER 6

Photograph of Hadberg's cabin. 1910. Courtesy Aberdeen Herald, *April 11, 1910.*

CHAPTER 8

Photograph of Billy Gohl. 1910. Courtesy Aberdeen Herald, *May 24, 1910.*

CHAPTER 9

Photograph of the jury. 1910. Courtesy Aberdeen Herald, *May 9, 1910.*

Photograph of piece of Hadberg's skin showing tattoo marks. 1910. Courtesy Aberdeen Herald, *May 9, 1910.*

Slingshot Books

Minneapolis

www.slingshotbooks.com

www.ingramcontent.com/pod-product-compliance
Lightning Source LLC
Chambersburg PA
CBHW051328220526
45468CB00004B/1543